# God's Ten Commandments for Kids

## Illustrated & Written by
## Colleena Roberts

Copyright © 2025 Colleena Roberts
All rights reserved.

No part of this book may be reproduced, stored in a retrieval system, or transmitted in any form or by any means—electronic, mechanical, photocopying, recording, or otherwise—without the prior written permission of the author, except in the case of brief quotations for reviews or educational use.

This book is a work of faith-based literature intended to educate and inspire children about the Ten Commandments. While great care has been taken to ensure biblical accuracy, the author assumes no responsibility for errors or omissions.

Illustrations Generated using AI

Cover Design by Colleena Roberts

Self-Published by Colleena Roberts
Printed in the United States of America

For inquiries, contact: Colleena.roberts@gmail.com

**Scripture References:**

Unless otherwise noted, all Scripture quotations are taken from the New International Version (NIV). The final quote on the closing page is from the King James Version (KJV).

First Edition

# Dedication

To my blessed children, *Nina & Jahnoy*

You are my greatest blessing and inspiration. May this book plant seeds of faith in your hearts and guide you to walk in God's love. Always remember, His wisdom will light your path, and His commandments will keep you strong. I pray you grow to know Him deeply and carry His truth with you always.

With all my love,

**Mommy**

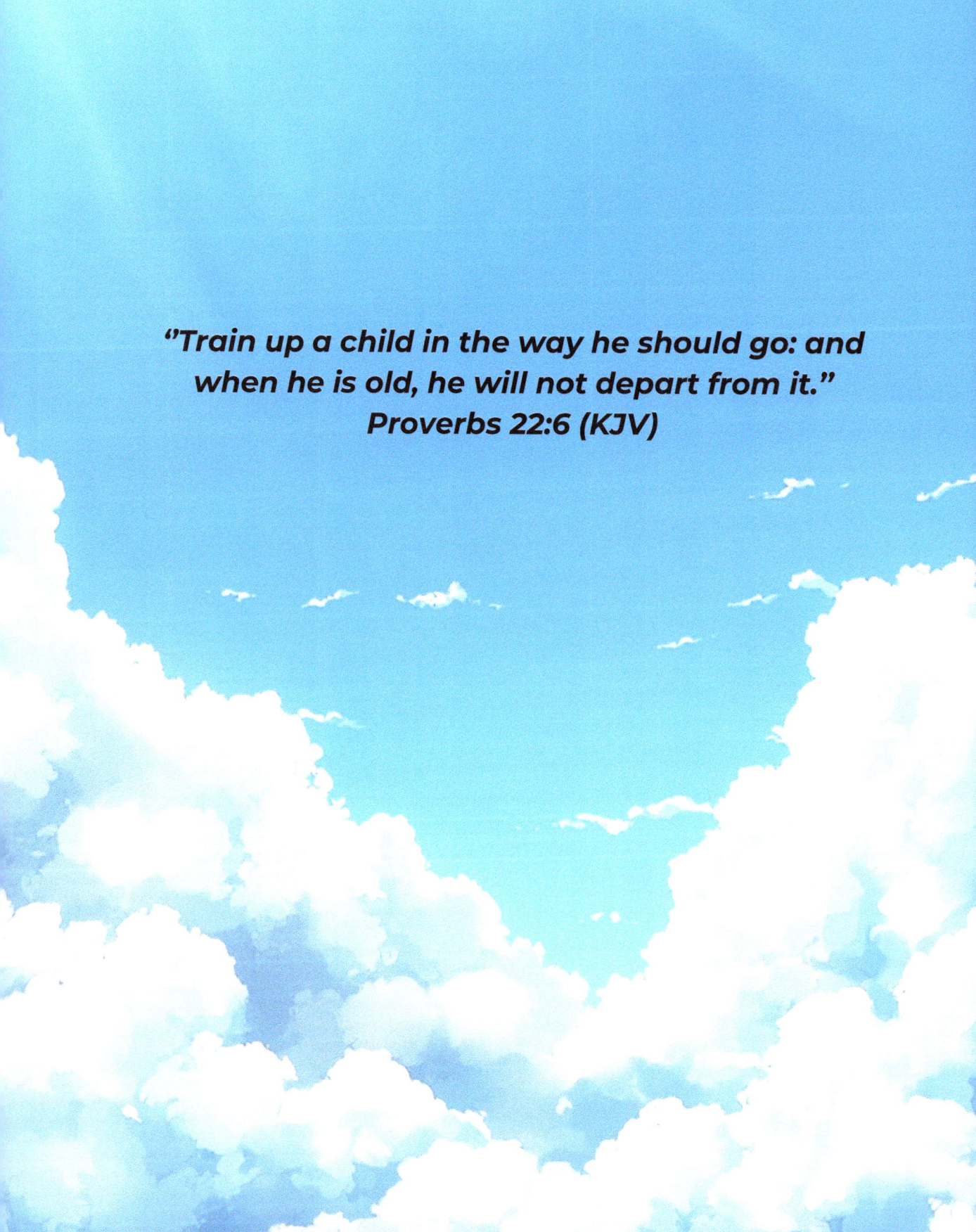

"Train up a child in the way he should go: and when he is old, he will not depart from it."
Proverbs 22:6 (KJV)

# First Commandment

**Love God First**

"You shall have no other gods before Me" –Exodus 20:3

**What does this mean?**

God wants to be the most important part of our lives! He loves us more than anything and wants us to love Him back.

# Third Commandment

"You shall not misuse the name of the Lord your God." – Exodus 20:7

**What does this mean?**

God's name is holy and powerful. We should use it with love and respect, not as a joke or when we're angry.

# Fifth Commandment

"Honor your father and your mother." – (Exodus 20:12)

## What This Means:

God wants us to respect and listen to our parents. They help guide us, love us, and teach us right from wrong. Honoring them means being kind, obeying their rules, and showing gratitude for all they do.

# Sixth Commandment

"You shall not murder." (Exodus 20:13)

**What This Means:**

God values every life, and He wants us to treat others with love and kindness. This commandment is not just about harming someone physically but also about our words and actions. When we speak with kindness and forgive others, we choose love over anger.

# Seventh Commandment

"You shall not commit adultery." — (Exodus 20:14)

**What This Means:**

God teaches us that love is a promise. Marriage is a special bond that should be honored with faithfulness, kindness, and trust. Keeping our promises to one another pleases God and helps build strong, happy families.

# Eighth Commandment

"You shall not STEAL." – (Exodus 20:15)

**What does this mean?**

We should respect what belongs to others and never take anything that isn't ours. Taking things without asking is stealing, and it's not loving or fair.

# Ninth Commandment

"You shall not give false testimony against your neighbor." – (Exodus 20:16)

What does this mean?

We should always tell the truth and be honest, because lying hurts others and breaks trust.

# Tenth Commandment

**What does this mean?**

Be happy with what you have because God has already given you wonderful things.

"Do not desire what belongs to someone else— their house, spouse, or anything they have."—Exodus 20:17

# A Special Message for You

Thank you for reading The 10 Commandments for Kids! I hope this book helps you understand how much God loves you and how He wants us to live with kindness, honesty, and love.

Remember, following God's commandments isn't about being perfect—it's about trying our best every day and trusting Him to guide us. Keep learning, keep growing, and always keep God first!

With love and blessings,
Colleena R.

# A Payer for You

**Dear God**,

Thank You for teaching us Your Ten Commandments. Help us to always follow Your ways and make good choices every day. Fill our hearts with kindness, honesty, and love for others. When we make mistakes, remind us that You are always ready to forgive us and guide us back to You.

Bless our families, our friends, and everyone who helps us learn more about You. Let Your light shine in our hearts so that we may grow in wisdom and always do what is right.

In Jesus' name, we pray,

**Amen**.

www.ingramcontent.com/pod-product-compliance
Ingram Content Group UK Ltd.
Pitfield, Milton Keynes, MK11 3LW, UK
UKHW061623240426
12048UKWH00050B/1700